WHAT'S UNDER THE GROUND?

Susan Mayes

Designed by Mike Pringle
Illustrated by Mike Pringle, Brin Edwards and John Scorey

CONTENTS

Under your feet

Under the ground there is a world you hardly ever see. Something is happening down there all the time.

People underground

People do different jobs under the ground. They dig and build, or mend things under the street. They even travel through specially made tunnels.

Animals

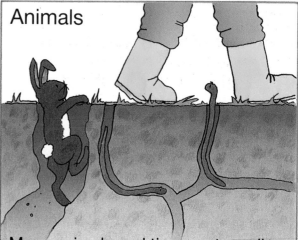

Many animals and tiny creatures live in the soil under your feet. Some of them come out to hunt or play. Others stay underground all the time.

Plants

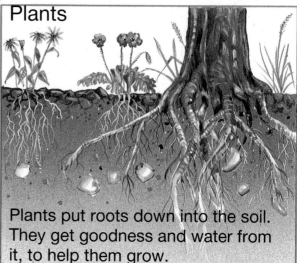

Plants put roots down into the soil. They get goodness and water from it, to help them grow.

Life long ago

The bones of huge creatures have been found under the ground. They were buried for millions of years.

Digging things up

Your home may be made from things which are dug out of the ground. So are lots of things you use every day.

Dinosaur skeletons have been uncovered in some countries. They show us what lived long ago.

There are many different things hidden under the ground. You can find out all about them in this book.

Under the street

Pipes, tunnels and cables are put under the street to keep them out of the way. You cannot see them most of the time, but there are clues which tell you they are there.

A metal plate on a wall shows that there is a big underground water pipe nearby.

Under the metal cover is a room called a manhole. Pipes go through it, carrying fresh water.

Rainwater runs through this grate. It goes down pipes which carry it away.

Water pipes
Fresh water for you to drink and use is pumped through the mains pipe.

mains pipe

Another pipe joins the mains and takes the water into your home.

Drains and sewers
A drain is a pipe which carries dirty water and waste from your house.

Then the waste runs into bigger pipes. They are called sewers.

Storm drains
Rainwater flows through a grate and fills a pit under the street.

Rubbish collects here.

The water runs into a pipe. This takes it to the storm drain.

Most telephone messages travel through underground cables.

When workers dig up the road you can often see electric cables or gas pipes under the ground.

Did you know?
Many telephone cables have thin glass threads inside. Your message goes along one of these.

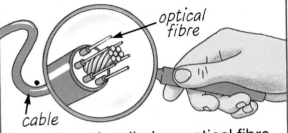

optical fibre

cable

Each thread, called an optical fibre, is as thin as a human hair. It can carry thousands of calls at one time.

Putting electricity underground
Electric cables carry power to homes, schools, factories, hospitals and shops. They often go underground.

First, deep trenches are dug in the street. Pipes called ducts are laid in them and covered with soil.

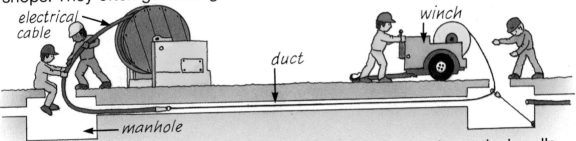

electrical cable

winch

duct

manhole

The electric cable is on a huge reel. One end is put down an electrical manhole and into the duct.

At the next manhole, a winch pulls the cable through. The end will be joined to a cable from another duct.

5

Tunnels for travel

Many cities in the world have underground railways. Thousands of people use them every day to get to places quickly and easily.

Building tunnels

The world's first underground railway was built in London, in 1863.

A huge trench was dug in the road. Railway lines were laid in it and covered with an arched roof. Then the road was built over the top again.

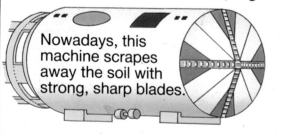

Nowadays, this machine scrapes away the soil with strong, sharp blades.

Today, tunnels are built much deeper under the ground. Machines can drill holes under buildings and rivers.

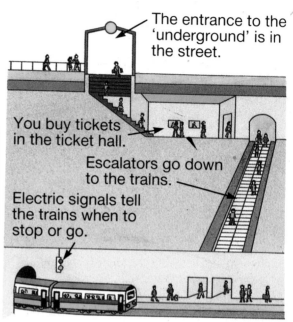

The entrance to the 'underground' is in the street.

You buy tickets in the ticket hall.

Escalators go down to the trains.

Electric signals tell the trains when to stop or go.

Did you know?

In some countries, road tunnels are built inside mountains. The longest one in the world is in Switzerland.

The St. Gotthard Road Tunnel goes through the Swiss Alps. It is just over 16 kilometres long.

The Channel Tunnel

The Channel Tunnel is really three tunnels. They will go under the sea between Britain and France.

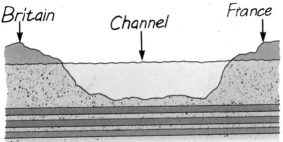

People in both countries are digging the tunnels through the hard chalk. They hope to finish work in 1993.

Trains will carry passengers through two of the tunnels. They must not go faster than 160 kilometres an hour.

In an accident, people could get out through this passage.

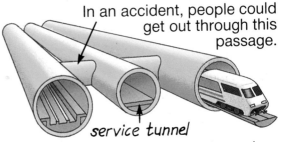

service tunnel

The middle tunnel is called a service tunnel. Workers will go through it when they make repairs.

Lining a tunnel

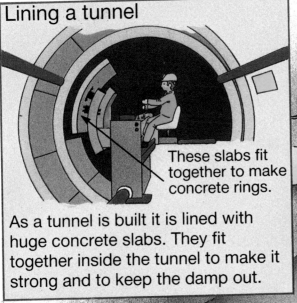

These slabs fit together to make concrete rings.

As a tunnel is built it is lined with huge concrete slabs. They fit together inside the tunnel to make it strong and to keep the damp out.

Electric cables are fixed to the tunnel walls. They work lights and machines.

Lorries, tractors and trucks drive around inside the tunnel.

7

Under your home

Some buildings have rooms underneath. A few homes are built underground. But nearly all buildings begin below the surface.

Building foundations

Builders make the foundations of a house first. These are built into the ground and the house is built on top. They stop the house from sinking.

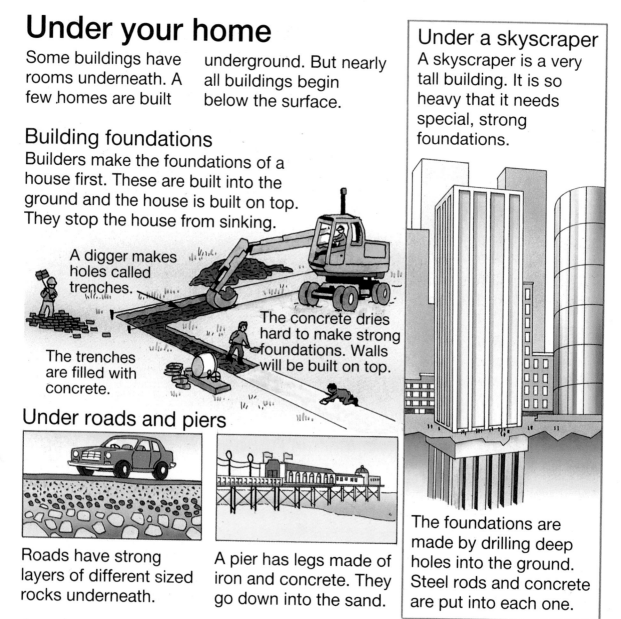

A digger makes holes called trenches.

The trenches are filled with concrete.

The concrete dries hard to make strong foundations. Walls will be built on top.

Under roads and piers

Roads have strong layers of different sized rocks underneath.

A pier has legs made of iron and concrete. They go down into the sand.

Under a skyscraper

A skyscraper is a very tall building. It is so heavy that it needs special, strong foundations.

The foundations are made by drilling deep holes into the ground. Steel rods and concrete are put into each one.

A city on water

Venice, in Italy, was built over a salty lake called a lagoon.

In Venice, people travel along canals.

Logs were pushed down into the muddy ground under the lagoon. Wood and stones were laid across the logs. The city was built on top.

Basements and cellars

Some buildings have rooms which are lower than the street. This underground part is the basement.

This is a wine cellar underneath a hotel.

A cellar is an underground room used for storing things. Wine is kept in a cellar as it is cool down there.

Underground homes

The Berber people live in Tunisia, Africa. They build underground homes.

The top rooms are used for storing things in.

The bottom rooms are for living in.

They find deep pits and burrow into the walls to make rooms. These stay cool in the hot daytime. On cold winter nights the rooms are warm.

Holes and burrows

Many animals tunnel down into the soil to make homes underground.

These homes are safe and hidden away. They have different names.

Badgers live in a home called a set. They rest there in the day and come out at night.

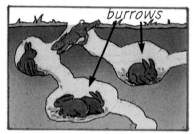

Lots of rabbits live together in a warren. It is made up of groups of burrows.

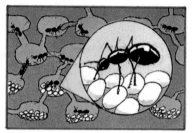

Ants live in an underground home called a nest. It is made of passages and rooms.

Made for digging

Burrowing animals have bodies which are very good at digging.

Moles have strong front legs. They can dig easily with their shovel-shaped feet.

Earthworms have strong muscles to pull them through the soil.

Rabbits use their front paws to burrow into the ground. They push the soil away with their back legs.

Moles live in the dark and are almost blind.

Living in hot places

Deserts are hot, dry places. Most small desert animals live in burrows in the daytime. They come out at night when the air is cooler.

The fennec fox hunts at night and rests in its burrow in the day.

The jerboa comes out to search for seeds and dry grass.

Keeping damp

An Australian desert frog sleeps in its burrow nearly all year.

A special covering of skin keeps it damp. It only comes out when it starts to rain.

Living in cold places

Animals live in some of the coldest places in the world. Many survive by eating a lot, then sleeping all winter. This is called hibernation.

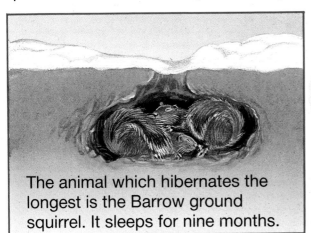

The animal which hibernates the longest is the Barrow ground squirrel. It sleeps for nine months.

Families of marmots hibernate inside their warm burrows. They make grass nests and block the way in.

What's in the soil?

Soil is really layers of stones, sand and clay. These come from rock which has been worn away by water and wind. This takes millions of years.

Nothing would grow without humus. This is made from dead plants and animals which have rotted away. The soil on top is full of humus.

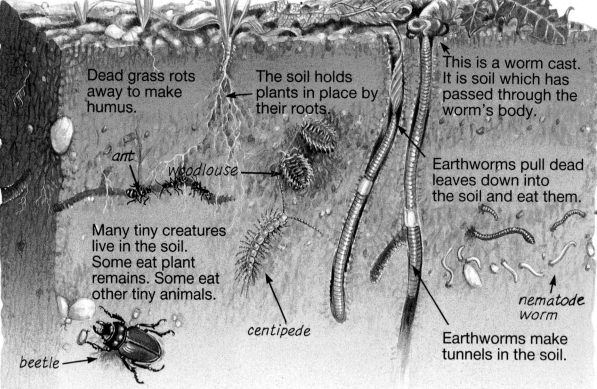

Dead grass rots away to make humus.

The soil holds plants in place by their roots.

This is a worm cast. It is soil which has passed through the worm's body.

ant

woodlouse

Earthworms pull dead leaves down into the soil and eat them.

Many tiny creatures live in the soil. Some eat plant remains. Some eat other tiny animals.

centipede

nematode worm

beetle

Earthworms make tunnels in the soil.

Humus changes into something called minerals. All living things need minerals to help them grow*. Minerals feed plants with goodness to make them strong. Earthworms help mix the minerals into the soil. Plants also need air and water. These get into the soil through tunnels made by worms.

Calcium is a mineral, for example. It makes your teeth and bones strong.

Making a wormery

Fill a jar with layers of soil and sand. Make sure the soil is damp, then put some leaves on top.

Cover the jar with a cloth.

Put a few worms in the jar, then cover it up so it is dark. The worms will start to tunnel. In a few days the soil and sand will be mixed up.

Wet and dry soil

Sandy soil is dry because water drains through it. Desert plants grow well in this kind of soil.

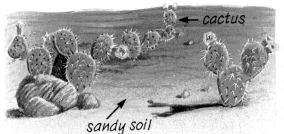

cactus

sandy soil

They would not grow in soil with lots of clay in it. Clay soil holds water easily. It is wet and sticky.

Food under the ground

Gardeners often grow plants in the same place every year. The minerals which feed the plants get used up.

beetroot

radishes

potatoes

carrots

compost heap

Many gardeners put goodness back into the soil by digging in compost. This is made from plants which have been specially left to rot away.

Vegetables grow well in dark, rich soil. The ones in this picture are root vegetables. This means that the part you eat grows under the ground.

All about fossils

Fossils are the remains of animals and plants which lived millions of years ago. This picture shows an animal which died and sank to the sea bed. The soft parts of its body rotted away, but the bones were left.

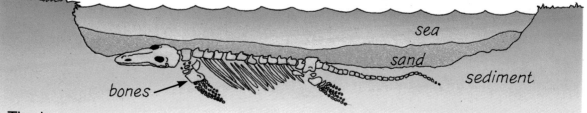

The bones were covered with sand and tiny grains called sediment. The sediment turned into hard rock and the bones were trapped inside.

Very slowly, minerals in the sediment changed the bones into fossils. These stayed buried for millions of years until the rocks were uncovered.

What fossils tell us

The fossils in these pictures helped scientists to guess what the first living things looked like.

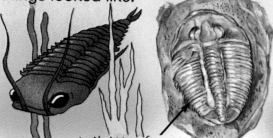

trilobite fossil

The first animals lived in water. Trilobites were sea creatures with hard bodies made of segments.

stegosaurus fossil

Later, dinosaurs ruled the Earth. A stegosaurus had bony plates on its back. Some plates were 1 metre high.

14

Plants long ago

This beautiful plant fossil is over 50 million years old.

Some kinds of sediment could save plant shapes for ever. There are many fossil remains of the first plants.

Looking for fossils

Fossil hunters do not usually find anything as huge as a dinosaur. But they do find lots of other fossils.

This special hammer helps to get the fossil out.

Rocky beaches are good places to search. A rock may get worn away and part of a fossil is uncovered.

arsinoitherium fossil

fossil of a footprint

Millions of years later there were animals almost like those we see now. This one was like a rhinoceros.

The very first kind of human lived about 4 million years ago. The oldest human fossils are from Africa.

Inside a cave

A cave is like an underground room. It is made by rainwater which wears rock away. Caves often form in limestone which wears away easily.

Water drips from the ceiling. It leaves minerals behind. Very slowly these begin to form rocky icicles called stalactites.

Drops with minerals in may hit the floor. They make rock towers called stalagmites.

An underground stream runs through this cave.

The water trickles down into holes and passages in the rock. It makes them bigger and bigger. A cave is a huge hole which has been made.

What lives in a cave?

Most animals living in the mouth of the cave also live in the outside world. Cave swallows fly in and out.

It is darker further inside. It is also damp and cool. Bats live here and come out to hunt at night.

Deep inside the cave it is dark all the time. Glow-worms may live in here. They make their own bright lights.

A hidden cave

The way into a cave is sometimes hidden. In 1940 two boys discovered a cave which no-one knew about.

The boys were walking their dog near Lascaux in France. They found the cave when the dog fell down the entrance which had bushes in front.

Cave paintings

The Lascaux cave has paintings on the ceiling and walls. Cave people did them thousands of years ago.

The cave people made their own paints and tools. They painted bulls, cows, deer, bison and horses. These were the animals they hunted.

Try this

Do a painting using tools and paints which you have made or found yourself. You will need:

Large scrap of paper or card   water   soil in a pot   twigs

You could also try painting using food dye in a few drops of water.

Mix a few drops of water into the soil. Cave people used coloured earth to make paint. They mostly used red, yellow, brown, black and white.

Dip the twig brush into the paint and try painting on the card with it. You may need to dip it in many times as you work, but keep going.

Useful things underground

People dig and drill for things far underground. Coal and oil help to make electricity, but they are also used to make lots of other things.

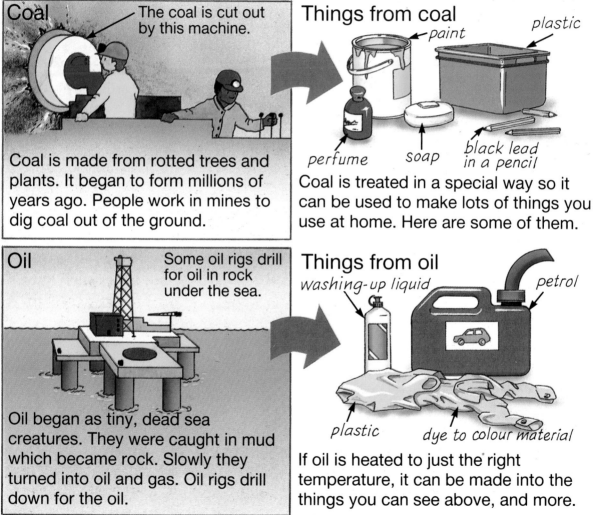

Coal

The coal is cut out by this machine.

Coal is made from rotted trees and plants. It began to form millions of years ago. People work in mines to dig coal out of the ground.

Things from coal

paint

plastic

perfume   soap

black lead in a pencil

Coal is treated in a special way so it can be used to make lots of things you use at home. Here are some of them.

Oil

Some oil rigs drill for oil in rock under the sea.

Oil began as tiny, dead sea creatures. They were caught in mud which became rock. Slowly they turned into oil and gas. Oil rigs drill down for the oil.

Things from oil

washing-up liquid

petrol

plastic

dye to colour material

If oil is heated to just the right temperature, it can be made into the things you can see above, and more.

Things for building

For thousands of years homes have been built using different kinds of rocks. They are dug out of the ground in places called quarries.

Clay is made from tiny grains of rock. Damp clay is made into shapes and baked hard to make tiles.

Glass is made by melting limestone, sand and something called soda.

Bricks are made from clay.

Building blocks are made of concrete.

Concrete is made from small stones, sand and cement. These are mixed with water and left to go hard. This makes a very strong building material.

Metal from the ground

Metal is found in rocks. You can find lots of metal things in your kitchen.

tin cans
cutlery
taps
oven
sink

Rock with metal in it is called ore. Some kinds of ore are heated in a special oven. The metal comes out as liquid ready for making things.

Did you know?

Jewels form deep inside the Earth where it is very hot. Minerals far underground turn into hard crystals.

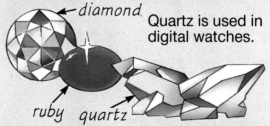

diamond

Quartz is used in digital watches.

ruby   quartz

These crystals are rough when they are taken out of the ground. They are cut and polished to make jewellery.

What's inside the Earth?

The Earth is like a ball with a hard, rocky crust. Some parts of the crust are weak and it often moves or cracks in these places.

Underneath the crust is the mantle. This is hot, soft rock which moves all the time.

crust

mantle

outer core

inner core

The middle of the Earth is called the core. The outside of the core is hot, runny metal. The inside is hard metal. This is the hottest part.

Sometimes the inside of the Earth moves so much that amazing things happen on the surface, where we live.

Volcanoes

A volcano is made when hot, runny rock is pushed up from inside the Earth. It hardens into a cone shape.

This volcano is erupting. Hot rock called lava is bursting out of it.

This lava will cool and harden into a layer of rock. The volcano gets bigger each time it erupts.

crater

Some cone-shaped mountains are old volcanoes. They are extinct. This means they do not erupt any more.

Shaking ground

An earthquake is when the ground shakes very hard. It happens when the Earth's crust moves suddenly.

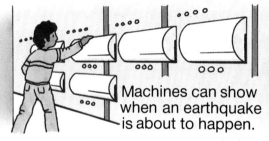

Machines can show when an earthquake is about to happen.

In countries with many earthquakes the buildings must be specially made, so they do not fall down.

Did you know?

In some places a fountain of hot water shoots out of the ground. It is called a geyser. The water is heated by hot rocks in the Earth's crust.

This geyser in America spouts water about once an hour.

In some countries they use underground heat to make electricity.

Buried treasure

Vesuvius is a volcano in Naples, Italy. It first erupted nearly two thousand years ago, in Roman times.

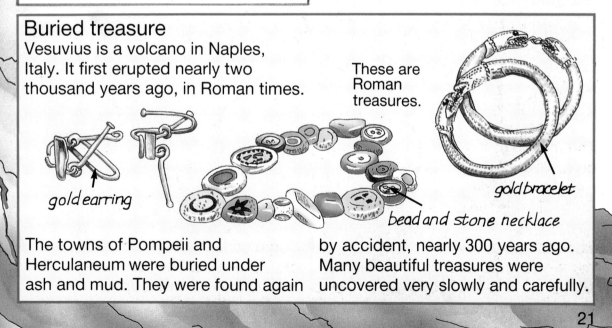

These are Roman treasures.

gold earring

bead and stone necklace

gold bracelet

The towns of Pompeii and Herculaneum were buried under ash and mud. They were found again by accident, nearly 300 years ago. Many beautiful treasures were uncovered very slowly and carefully.

Underground facts

On this page you can find out about some amazing things underground.

The longest tunnel
The world's longest tunnel is almost 169 kilometres long. It carries water to New York City, North America.

It is just over 4 metres high. That is about as high as two tall people.

The first bird
A fossil of the first bird that ever lived was dug up in Germany, in 1861. The bird was called Archaeopteryx. It lived over 150 million years ago. You can even see the feathers on the wings and body.

Going down

A man went almost 4 kilometres down into the ground in a mine in South Africa. This is the deepest that anyone has ever been.

The biggest cave
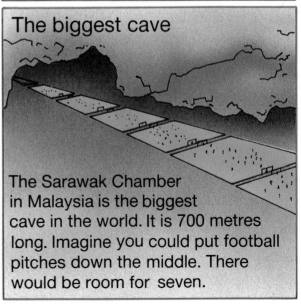

The Sarawak Chamber in Malaysia is the biggest cave in the world. It is 700 metres long. Imagine you could put football pitches down the middle. There would be room for seven.

Things to do

Real fossils take millions of years to form underground. You can make a model of a fossil for yourself.

You will need:

a lump of plasticine

a bag of modelling plaster from a model shop

a jug of water

an old bowl and spoon

some shells, bumpy stones or a fossil

Digging for creatures

Use a spade to dig into a patch of garden or waste ground. How many different creatures can you dig up?

Put them in a plastic box. Draw them and try to find out what they are. Afterwards, put them back again.

Flatten the plasticine a bit, then press a shell into it. Do not press it in too far. Take the shell out very carefully.

You could do the same with a stone or a fossil.

Put two handfuls of plaster into the bowl. Add a little water at a time and mix it in. The plaster is ready to use when it drips from the spoon.

Spoon the plaster into the hole in the plasticine. Leave it for 10 minutes to go hard. Peel away the plasticine to find the shell fossil.

Index